"Unlocking your ultimate self"

"Discovering Your Inner Potential and Transforming Your Life"

Godson henry

Introduction

"Unlocking Your Ultimate Self" is a transformative journey that explores the depths of our being and the potential for personal growth and fulfillment. This book is a guide for those seeking to uncover their true selves and unleash their full potential. Through engaging stories, exercises, and reflective prompts, the author guides readers on a journey of self-discovery, personal growth, and transformation. The purpose of this book is to empower readers to overcome the limitations and obstacles that are holding them back, and to help them tap into their inner strength, wisdom, and courage. Whether you're seeking personal growth, seeking to live a more fulfilling life, or looking to unlock your full potential, "Unlocking Your Ultimate Self" provides the tools, guidance, and inspiration needed to unleash your inner potential and live the life you were meant to live.

Chapter I

Understanding the concept of ultimate self

the concept of ultimate self is a deeply personal and philosophical understanding of one's true essence and purpose in life. It is the belief that each individual has a unique set of qualities, skills, and experiences that make up their core being, and that it is their responsibility to uncover and cultivate these traits in order to achieve a state of self-realization and fulfillment.

At the core of this concept is the belief that our true selves are buried beneath the layers of societal and cultural expectations, personal traumas, and external influences. To reach our ultimate self, we must work to peel back these layers and uncover our true innermost desires, passions, and values.

This process can involve exploring one's own thoughts and emotions, reflecting on past experiences, and engaging in activities that bring joy and fulfillment. It also involves a deep and honest look at the ways in which we have suppressed or denied our true selves, and the steps we need to take in order to release these parts of us.

Ultimately, reaching the ultimate self is a lifelong journey that requires patience, courage, and self-discovery. It is a journey that is unique to each individual and can bring a sense of peace, clarity, and purpose.

In order to fully understand the concept of ultimate self, it is important to be mindful and present in each moment, to be open to new experiences and perspectives, and to always be willing to explore and challenge our own beliefs and assumptions.

Reaching the ultimate self is not an easy or straightforward path, but it is one that can bring a sense of deep fulfillment and meaning to our lives. By embracing this concept and committing to the journey of self-discovery, we can gain a deeper understanding of who we truly are and what our purpose in life is.

Chapter II

.Understanding Yourself

Knowing your value

Understanding your ultimate self and knowing your ultimate values can be a complex and introspective process, but it is also an important step in personal growth and fulfillment. Here are a few tips to help you understand and identify your core values:

<u>Reflect on your life experiences:</u> Think about the experiences and situations that have had the most impact on your life and what values were most important to you in those moments. This will give you an idea of what values you hold dear.

<u>Identify your passions:</u> Consider what you are passionate about and what values are at the root of those passions.

For example, if you are passionate about helping others, the value of compassion might be a core value for you.

<u>Consider your beliefs</u>: Your beliefs are closely tied to your values. Consider what you believe to be true and important and how those beliefs inform your values.

<u>Look at your behavior:</u> Observe your own behavior and see what values are reflected in your actions. For example, if you consistently put others before yourself, the value of altruism might be important to you.

<u>Identify your priorities:</u> Take a moment to consider what is most important to you in life. What values do these priorities reflect?

Once you have identified your core values, it is important to keep them in mind and make decisions that align with them. Living a life in line with your values will bring a sense of purpose and fulfillment. Remember that your values may change over time as you grow and evolve, and that is okay. Regular self-reflection and exploration can help you stay in tune with your ultimate self and values.

Identifying your strengths and weaknesses

Identifying your ultimate self strengths and weaknesses is a crucial step in personal development and growth. Knowing what you are good at and what you need to improve upon can help you to focus your efforts in the right direction and achieve your goals.

Step 1: Reflect on your past experiences
Think about your past experiences, both personal and professional, and try to identify patterns of success and failure. What have you been able to achieve in the past, and what have you struggled with? This can help you to identify areas where you are naturally talented and where you need improvement.

Step 2: Seek feedback from others

Another way to identify your strengths and weaknesses is to ask for feedback from people who know you well. This can include friends, family members, coworkers, or mentors. Ask them what they think your greatest strengths and weaknesses are, and take their feedback into consideration when evaluating yourself.

Step 3: Take a personality test
Personality tests such as the Myers-Briggs Type Indicator (MBTI) can provide valuable insights into your strengths and weaknesses. These tests help you to understand your preferred way of thinking and behaving, and can help you to identify areas where you may struggle.

Step 4: Set goals for self-improvement
Once you have identified your strengths and weaknesses, set achievable goals for self-improvement. Focus on one or two areas where you would like to improve, and make a plan for how you will achieve those goals. This could involve taking courses, reading books, or seeking help from others.

Step 5: Monitor your progress

Finally, regularly monitor your progress and evaluate your success in achieving your goals. This will help you to see the results of your efforts and determine if you need to make any changes to your approach.

In conclusion, identifying your ultimate self strengths and weaknesses is an important step in personal development and growth. By reflecting on your past experiences, seeking feedback from others, taking personality tests, setting goals, and monitoring your progress, you can develop a better understanding of yourself and make the most of your potential.

Accepting your limitations

Accepting your limitations is an important step in personal growth and development. It allows you to focus on what you can do and how you can improve, rather than dwelling on what you cannot do. Here are some tips for accepting your limitations:

Acknowledge your limitations – Identifying what you cannot do is the first step in accepting them. This can be difficult, but it is important to be honest with yourself about your abilities.

Embrace your strengths – Instead of focusing on what you cannot do, focus on what you can do well. This will guide you to build your confidence and you will also guide feel great about yourself.

Set realistic goals – When setting goals, make sure they are achievable and within your limitations. This will help you to stay motivated and avoid disappointment.

Ask for help – Don't be afraid to ask for help when you need it. Accepting your limitations means admitting that you may need assistance to achieve your goals.

<u>Focus on growth and improvement</u> – Rather than focusing on what you cannot do, focus on how you can grow and improve. This will help you to develop new skills and reach your full potential.

Accept the things you cannot change – Some limitations are beyond your control, such as physical or mental disabilities. Accepting these limitations does not mean giving up, but rather finding alternative ways to achieve your goals.

In resolution, accepting your limitations is an important step in personal growth and development. It allows you to focus on what you can do and how you can improve, rather than dwelling on what you cannot do. Embrace your strengths, set realistic goals, ask for help, focus on growth and improvement, and accept the things you cannot change.

<u>Cultivating self-awareness</u>

Self-awareness is the key to unlocking one's full potential, improving relationships, and creating a more fulfilling life. Cultivating self-awareness is a journey that requires dedication, patience, and an open mind. Here are some steps to help you cultivate your ultimate self-awareness:

Observe your thoughts and emotions - Take some time to reflect on your thoughts and emotions throughout the day. Notice how your thoughts and emotions affect your behavior and decisions. Pay attention to how you react to different situations, and try to identify patterns in your thoughts and emotions.

<u>Practice mindfulness</u> - Mindfulness is a powerful tool for self-awareness. It involves being fully present in the moment and paying attention to your thoughts, emotions, and physical sensations. Practice mindfulness through meditation, yoga, or simply focusing on your breath for a few minutes each day.

<u>Journal</u> - Writing down your thoughts and emotions can be a great way to increase self-awareness. Keeping a journal allows you to reflect on your experiences and gain insight into your thoughts and emotions.

<u>Seek feedback</u> - Ask friends and family for their perspective on your behavior and attitudes. Seek out constructive criticism, and use it to improve your self-awareness.

<u>Engage in introspection</u> - Take some time to reflect on your beliefs, values, and priorities. Ask yourself why you believe what you believe, and consider if your beliefs align with your values and goals.

<u>Try new experiences</u> - Stepping outside of your comfort zone and trying new experiences can increase self-awareness. This can help you gain new perspectives and learn more about yourself.

<u>Use of self-compassion</u> - Be goodhearted and compassionate to yourself. Accept your flaws and mistakes, and focus on your strengths and successes.

finally, cultivating self-awareness requires a commitment to personal growth and introspection. Take small steps every day to increase your self-awareness, and you'll be well on your way to creating a more fulfilling life.

Chapter III

. <u>Overcoming Limiting Beliefs</u>

<u>Limiting beliefs</u>;are often seen as mental roadblocks that can prevent you from reaching your full potential. These beliefs are usually learned early in life and can be difficult to shake, but with effort and dedication, they can be overcome. In order to overcome limiting beliefs, you first need to recognize them, understand the impact they have on your life, and then implement techniques for breaking free from them.

<u>Recognizing negative thought patterns</u>;is the first step to overcoming limiting beliefs. Negative thought patterns are often self-defeating and can prevent you from reaching your full potential. Some common negative thought patterns include, self-doubt, negative self-talk, and an obsession with perfectionism. To recognize these thought patterns, you must be aware of your thoughts and how they affect your behavior and emotions.

<u>The impact of limiting beliefs;</u> on your life can be significant. These beliefs can prevent you from pursuing your passions, taking risks, and pursuing your goals. Limiting beliefs can also impact your confidence, self-esteem, and overall mental health. Understanding the impact of these beliefs can help you understand the importance of breaking free from them.

There are several techniques that you can use to break free from limiting beliefs. One of the most effective techniques is self-reflection. Self-reflection involves taking time to reflect on your thoughts, beliefs, and behaviors and understanding how they impact your life. Another technique is visualization. Visualization involves imagining yourself as the person you want to be, with the belief system and qualities that you desire. This can help to reprogram your mind and create new, positive beliefs.

To build a growth mindset for your ultimate self, it is important to focus on self-development and learning. This involves setting personal and professional goals, developing new skills, and seeking out new challenges and experiences. A growth mindset requires a focus on continuous improvement and the belief that you can always grow and develop, no matter what your current circumstances are.

In conclusion, overcoming limiting beliefs requires effort and dedication, but it is possible. By recognizing negative thought patterns, understanding the impact of limiting beliefs, and implementing techniques for breaking free, you can build a growth mindset that will allow you to reach your full potential and achieve your goals

ChapterIV

Enhancing Your Emotional Intelligence

Enhancing your emotional intelligence is a journey that involves understanding, managing, and regulating your emotions and those of others. Emotional intelligence is the capacity to be aware of, control, and express one's emotions, and to handle interpersonal relationships judiciously and empathetically. Here are a few ways to enhance your emotional intelligence:

Understanding Emotions: To enhance your emotional intelligence, it is crucial to understand the different emotions that you and others experience. Emotions can be positive or negative, and it is essential to understand the difference. Understanding emotions will help you to recognize and acknowledge your own emotions and those of others.

Identifying and Managing Emotions: Once you have a good understanding of emotions, it is time to learn how to identify and manage your own emotions and those of others. When you are aware of your emotions, you can manage them in a healthy and productive way. This will help you to maintain emotional balance and avoid unnecessary conflicts.

Building Empathy and Compassion: Empathy and compassion are essential components of emotional intelligence. Empathy is the ability to understand and share the feelings of others, while compassion is the ability to act with kindness and concern for others. To build empathy and compassion, you can practice active listening, put yourself in their' shoes, and show genuine concern for others.

<u>Developing Emotional Resilience</u>: Emotional resilience is the ability to bounce back from negative emotions and challenging situations. To develop emotional resilience, it is important to practice self-care, set boundaries, and seek support from others when needed. Emotional resilience is a crucial component of emotional intelligence, as it helps you to manage stress and cope with adversity.

Lastly, enhancing your emotional intelligence requires effort and dedication, but it is worth it. By understanding, managing, and regulating your emotions and those of others, you can improve your relationships, enhance your communication skills, and lead a happier and more fulfilling life.

Chapter V

. Mindfulness and Meditation

<u>Understanding Mindfulness</u>

Mindfulness is state of being conscious or aware of something and accepting one's emotions, thoughts, and bodily commotion. It is a form of self-awareness that helps one to be more mindful of the present moment and the world around them. Mindfulness allows individuals to focus their attention on the present moment and experience things in a non-judgmental and accepting way. It is a mental state that encourages one to be more aware of their thoughts, emotions, and physical sensations, allowing them to become more attuned to their own inner workings.

<u>Benefits of Mindfulness</u>

There are numerous benefits associated with practicing mindfulness, including:

Reducing stress and anxiety

Improving emotional regulation

Boosting cognitive abilities, such as memory and focus

Strengthening the immune system

Promoting self-awareness and personal growth

Improving overall well-being

C. Techniques for Practicing Mindfulness

There are many different techniques that individuals can use to practice mindfulness, including:

Deep breathing exercises

Body scanning meditation

Sensory awareness meditation

Mindful walking

Mantra repetition

Loving-kindness meditation

The Importance of Meditation in Self-Discovery

Meditation is an integral part of mindfulness practice and is essential for self-discovery. By meditating, individuals can gain a deeper understanding of their thoughts, emotions, and physical sensations. They can also acquire understanding of their mental processes and acquire the ability to reframe their thoughts and let go of negative thoughts and emotions. Meditation allows individuals to quiet their minds and become more attuned to their inner selves, leading to a greater sense of self-awareness and personal growth. By regularly meditating, individuals can deepen their mindfulness practice and gain a greater understanding of themselves and the world around them.

Chapter VI

Building Strong Relationships

Understanding and managing conflict

Building strong relationships is a key aspect of life. It allows us to connect with others and create meaningful connections that can lead to happiness, growth, and success. In this article, we will discuss the importance of relationships and provide tips on how to build strong relationships, communicate effectively, cultivate positive relationships, and manage conflicts.

The Importance of Relationships

Relationships play a critical role in our lives. They provide us with love, support, and a sense of belonging. They also help us grow and learn new things, while allowing us to be ourselves. Strong relationships also have a positive impact on our health and well-being, leading to lower levels of stress, anxiety, and depression.

Building Strong Relationships

Building strong relationships requires effort, patience, and a willingness to understand others. Here are some tips to help you build strong relationships:

Be Honest and Open: Being honest and open about your feelings, thoughts, and actions is critical to building trust and strong relationships.

Listen and Empathize: Listening to others and trying to understand their perspective is key to building strong relationships. Empathy and understanding are essential to building strong relationships.

Show Appreciation: Expressing appreciation and gratitude towards others is essential to building strong relationships. This helps to build trust and strengthens the connection between people.

Share Experiences: Sharing experiences and common interests helps to build strong relationships and create bonds.

Be Respectful: Respecting others and their opinions is key to building strong relationships. This includes listening to their views and avoiding negative or hurtful comments.

Building Strong Communication Skills

Strong communication skills are key to building and maintaining strong relationships. Here are some tips to help you improve your communication skills:

<u>Be Clear</u>: Be clear and concise when communicating, and avoid using complex language or ambiguity.

<u>Listen</u>: Listen actively to others and show that you are paying attention. This helps to build trust and strengthens relationships.

<u>Ask Questions</u>: Asking questions and seeking clarification shows that you are engaged and interested in what the other person is saying.

<u>Avoid Assumptions</u>: Avoid making assumptions about others and their intentions. This helps to avoid misunderstandings and conflicts.

<u>Be Empathetic:</u> Show empathy and understanding when communicating with others. This helps to build trust and strengthen relationships.

<u>Cultivating Positive Relationships</u>

Cultivating positive relationships requires effort and a positive mindset. Here are some tips to help you cultivate positive relationships:

<u>Be Positive</u>: Focus on the positive aspects of others and your relationship with them. This helps to create a positive atmosphere and strengthens relationships.

<u>Be Supportive</u>: Be supportive of others and their goals. This helps to build trust and strengthen relationships.

<u>Practice Forgiveness:</u> Forgive others for their mistakes and move on. Holding onto negative feelings can harm relationships and prevent growth.

<u>Be Emotional</u>: Show your emotions and be open about how you feel. This helps to build trust and strengthen relationships.

<u>Share Your Life</u>: Share your life with others and let them get to know you. This helps to build trust and strengthen relationships.

Understand and Managing Conflict

Conflict is an inevitable part of life and can arise in any type of relationship or situation. Understanding how to effectively manage conflict can help to resolve disputes and prevent them from escalating.

The first step in managing conflict is to understand the root cause of the issue. Often, conflicts arise from misunderstandings, conflicting needs, or competing interests. To understand the root cause, it's important to take a step back and look at the situation objectively. Try to identify the underlying concerns and needs of all parties involved.

Once the root cause has been identified, the next step is to communicate effectively. Good communication skills are essential in conflict resolution. Listen actively to the concerns of others and be open to their perspective. Avoid blaming and name-calling, and instead focus on finding common ground and a solution that works for everyone.

It's also important to be flexible and willing to compromise. In most conflicts, both sides will have to make some concessions in order to reach a resolution. A willingness to compromise shows that you are open-minded and willing to work together to find a solution.

Another effective technique for managing conflict is to use negotiation and problem-solving skills. This involves exploring different options and finding a solution that meets the needs of all parties involved. Be creative and think outside the box when it comes to finding solutions.

Finally, it's important to understand the impact that emotions can have on conflict. Emotions can escalate conflicts and make it more difficult to resolve them. To avoid this, try to keep your emotions in check and avoid getting defensive or reactive. If necessary, take a step back and give yourself time to calm down before continuing the discussion.

Therefore, conflict can be a challenging and emotional experience, but with the right approach, it can also be a valuable opportunity for growth and improvement. By understanding the root cause, communicating effectively, being flexible and compromising, using negotiation and problem-solving skills, and managing your emotions, you can effectively manage conflict and resolve disputes.

ChapterVII

. Pursuing Your Passions

Pursuing your passions can bring a sense of purpose and fulfillment to your life. However, it can be challenging to know how to turn your passions into a reality. Here are some steps to help you pursue your ultimate self passions:

<u>Identify your passions</u>: This may seem like an obvious step, but it's important to take some time to reflect on what truly excites you. Think about what you enjoy doing, what you find meaningful, and what you're naturally good at. Explore new opportunities and test them out to discover what connects with your interests and passions.

<u>Set realistic goals</u>:At the moment that you have recognized your own areas of interest or things you love, establish attainable objectives or targets which shall aid oneself in following those interests. For example, if you're passionate

about photography, your goal might be to take a photography course or to enter a photography contest.

Create a plan of action: Rephrase your objectives into smaller, achievable actions.Reorganize your daily routine and adhere to it consistently You can also seek out resources and support from others who have similar passions.

Surround yourself with supportive people: Surrounding yourself with supportive friends, family, and mentors can help you stay motivated and inspired as you pursue your passions. Find a community of like-minded individuals who will encourage you and provide you with the support you need.

Stay committed: Pursuing your passions requires a lot of hard work and dedication. Stay focused and remain committed to your goals, even when things get tough. Remember why you started and how pursuing your passions will make you feel fulfilled.

<u>Be happy about your successes</u>: It's important to commemorate your accomplishments, even if they are minor. Recognize your achievements and reward yourself for your hard work. This will help you stay motivated and continue pursuing your passions with even more enthusiasm.

Pursuing your passions takes time and effort, but the rewards are well worth it. When you're doing what you love, you'll feel a sense of purpose and fulfillment that can positively impact all areas of your life.

Identifying your passions

Identifying your ultimate passion can be a difficult and time-consuming task, but it is essential to find happiness and purpose in life. Here are some steps you can follow to identify your ultimate person passion:

<u>Reflect on your interests:</u> Start by exploring your interests and hobbies. What do you enjoy doing in your free time? What do you find yourself naturally drawn towards? These activities may be a good starting point for identifying your passion.

<u>Analyze your skills</u>: Think about the skills you possess. What are you naturally good at? What tasks come easily to you? Your skills can provide clues as to what your passion might be.

<u>Consider your values</u>: Your values play a significant role in what you find fulfilling. Think about what values you hold important, such as creativity, challenge, or helping others.

<u>Ask for opinions</u>: Talk to people who know you well and ask for their thoughts on what they think your passions

might be. This can provide you with a new perspective and open up new possibilities.

Try new things: Don't be afraid to try new things. Join a club, take a class, or volunteer for an organization. This will give you the opportunity to explore different activities and find out what you enjoy.

Follow your intuition: Trust your instincts. If something feels right, it probably is. Your intuition can guide you towards your ultimate passion.

Keep an open mind: Your ultimate passion may not be what you initially expect. Keep an open mind and be willing to consider new possibilities.

Identifying your ultimate passion may take time, but the journey can be an exciting and fulfilling one. Remember to be patient and keep exploring until you find something that brings you joy and purpose

<u>Overcoming fear and doubt</u>

Fear and doubt can be two of the biggest obstacles in life that prevent us from reaching our full potential. But with a little effort and the right approach, these feelings can be overcome. Here are some steps that can help you overcome fear and doubt:

Identify the source of your fear and doubt: The first step in overcoming fear and doubt is to understand what is causing them. Are you afraid of failure? Are you uncertain about your abilities? Once you have identified the source of your fear and doubt, you can start to work on overcoming them.

Challenge negative thoughts: Our thoughts have a powerful impact on our emotions and actions. If you find yourself thinking negative thoughts, try to challenge them. Ask yourself if they are true, and if not, replace them with more positive thoughts.

<u>Practice self-care</u>: When we're feeling overwhelmed with fear and doubt, it's important to take care of ourselves. Engage in activities that bring you joy and relaxation, and try to avoid situations that trigger your fear and doubt.

<u>Set realistic goals</u>: Setting achievable goals can help you overcome fear and doubt. When you reach small milestones, it can give you a sense of accomplishment and increase your confidence.

Surround yourself with positive people: Being around people who support and encourage you can help boost your confidence and reduce fear and doubt. Surround yourself with positive, uplifting people who will help you stay motivated and inspired.

Practice visualization: Visualization is a powerful tool that can help you overcome fear and doubt. Close your eyes and imagine yourself successfully overcoming your fears. See yourself as confident and capable. Repeat this visualization as often as you need to.

Take action: The best way to overcome fear and doubt is to take action. Don't let your fears hold you back, instead, take small steps towards your goals. The more you face your fears, the less daunting they will become.

In conclusion, fear and doubt can be debilitating, but they can be overcome with effort and the right approach. By focusing on self-care, setting realistic goals, surrounding yourself with positive people, practicing visualization, and taking action, you can overcome your fears and doubts and reach your full potential

Building a plan for pursuing your passions

Building a plan for pursuing your ultimate passions can be a life-changing experience, but it requires careful consideration and planning. Here are some steps to help you get started:

Identify your passions: Take some time to reflect on what truly makes you happy and fulfilled. Ask yourself what you would do if you had unlimited time and resources. This will give you a good starting point for your plan.

Prioritize your passions: Once you have a list of your passions, it's time to prioritize them. Consider which ones are most important to you and which ones would have the greatest impact on your life if you were to pursue them.

Set goals: Determine what you want to achieve with each passion. For example, if your passion is writing, you may want to write a book or start a blog. Be specific and set realistic goals that you can work towards.

Create a timeline: Set a deadline for each goal and break it down into smaller, more manageable steps. This will help you stay on track and make progress towards your ultimate goal.

Make a budget: Pursuing your passions often requires financial resources. Create a budget for your plan, taking into account the cost of supplies, travel, and any other expenses that may be involved.

Seek support: Surround yourself with people who will support and encourage you. This may be family, friends, or even a mentor. They can help you stay motivated and offer advice when you need it.

Stay focused: Pursuing your passions can be a long and challenging journey, but it is important to stay focused and committed. Keep your end goal in mind and remind yourself why it is important to you.

By following these steps, you can build a plan for pursuing your ultimate passions. Remember that the journey may be difficult at times, but the reward will be worth it.

Overcoming obstacles and setbacks

Overcoming obstacles and setbacks is a critical component of success. Whether you're working towards personal or professional goals, you will inevitably face challenges along the way. But, it's how you respond to those challenges that will ultimately determine your success. Here are some tips to help you overcome obstacles and setbacks:

<u>Develop a Growth Mindset</u>: Adopt a growth mindset, which means viewing challenges as opportunities for growth and improvement. When faced with obstacles, instead of giving up, focus on how you can learn from the experience and use it to grow.

Stay Positive: Maintaining a positive outlook, even in the face of setbacks, is crucial. Surround yourself with positive people and focus on the things you're grateful for in your life.

Set Realistic Goals: Establishing realistic goals can help you stay motivated and focused. Make sure your goals are specific, measurable, attainable, relevant, and time-bound.

Get Organized: When facing obstacles, it's essential to be organized. Write down your goals, create a plan of action, and take concrete steps towards your objectives.

Be Adaptable: Be prepared to adapt to change and modify your approach when necessary. Sometimes, what worked in the past may not work in the present, so be open to new ideas and approaches.

Stay Focused: It's easy to get discouraged when faced with obstacles, but it's important to stay focused on your goals. Keep a positive attitude and focus on what you can control.

<u>Seek Support</u>: Don't try to overcome obstacles and setbacks alone. Reach out to friends, family, or a mentor for support and guidance.

In conclusion, overcoming obstacles and setbacks is a critical component of success. By developing a growth mindset, staying positive, setting realistic goals, getting organized, being adaptable, staying focused, and seeking support, you can overcome any challenge that comes your way. Remember, setbacks and obstacles are simply opportunities for growth and improvement.

Chapter VIII

. Finding Inner Peace

We must understand that inner peace is a state of tranquility and calmness within oneself. So finding your ultimate self and unlocking inner peace can be a journey of self-discovery and growth. It involves connecting with your innermost desires, values, and beliefs, and aligning them with your thoughts, words, and actions. Here are some steps to help you find and unlock your ultimate self and inner peace:

<u>Practice mindfulness</u>: Mindfulness is the practice of being present and aware of the moment without judgment. It can help you gain insight into your thoughts, feelings, and emotions, and help you find a sense of calm.

<u>Reflect on your values and beliefs</u>: Spend time exploring your core values and beliefs, and assess whether your actions align with them. This can help you understand

what truly matters to you, and give you a sense of purpose and direction.

Embrace change: Embracing change and stepping outside of your comfort zone can help you grow and expand your understanding of the world. It can also help you find new ways of approaching challenges, and help you find your own voice.

Practice self-care: Taking care of your physical, mental, and emotional health is crucial for finding inner peace. This can include activities like exercise, meditation, and spending time in nature.

Surround yourself with positive people: Surrounding yourself with positive and supportive people can help you feel more connected and empowered. It can also help you find a sense of community, and provide you with a support system.

Unlocking your ultimate self and inner peace can be a lifelong journey, but it is worth it. When you connect with your innermost desires, values, and beliefs, you can experience a greater sense of peace and purpose in your life.

.<u>Understanding the important of inner</u> peace

Inner peace is a feeling of contentment, balance and harmony that can help reduce stress and anxiety. Understanding the importance of inner peace is crucial for leading a fulfilling and meaningful life.

The first step in understanding the importance of inner peace is to recognize the impact of stress and negative emotions on our daily lives. When we are constantly stressed and anxious, it affects our physical and mental health, our relationships, and our ability to perform daily tasks. This can lead to a cycle of constant worry, which can make it difficult to achieve inner peace.

Another way to understand the importance of inner peace is to think about how it helps us in our relationships with others. When we are in a state of inner peace, we are more patient, compassionate, and understanding. We are also better able to handle conflicts and disagreements in a calm and rational manner.

Moreover, inner peace helps us to focus on the present moment. It allows us to be mindful and aware of our thoughts and emotions, and to appreciate the beauty and joy in our daily lives. This helps us to cultivate gratitude and contentment, which can bring a sense of meaning and purpose to our lives.

In order to achieve inner peace, it is important to adopt habits and practices that promote self-care and relaxation. This may include meditation, yoga, exercise, or spending time in nature. It is also helpful to engage in activities that bring us joy and happiness, such as hobbies, spending time with loved ones, or volunteering.

In conclusion, inner peace is an essential component of a healthy and fulfilling life. By understanding the importance of inner peace, we can take steps to cultivate this state of mind and enjoy the benefits it brings. Whether it be through self-care practices or mindfulness exercises, the key is to make inner peace a priority and to make it a part of our daily lives.

<u>Techniques for finding inner</u>

Finding inner peace is a personal journey and can be achieved through various techniques. Here are a few popular ones:

<u>Meditation</u>: Meditation is a powerful tool for calming the mind and finding inner peace. It involves focusing on the present moment, and observing one's thoughts without judgment. Regular meditation practice has been shown to reduce stress, anxiety, and depression, and can lead to greater feelings of inner peace and contentment.

<u>Mindfulness:</u> Mindfulness is a state of awareness that involves being present in the moment and paying attention to one's thoughts, feelings, and sensations. Practicing mindfulness can help you become more aware of your

thoughts and feelings, which can lead to a greater sense of inner peace.

Yoga: Yoga is a physical and mental practice that can help you find inner peace. By combining physical postures, breathing exercises, and meditation, yoga can help you become more aware of your body and mind, and reduce stress and anxiety.

Journaling: Writing about your thoughts and feelings can be a helpful tool for finding inner peace. By reflecting on your experiences, you can gain a better understanding of your emotions and identify any negative thought patterns that may be contributing to feelings of stress and anxiety.

Gratitude Practice: Taking time each day to reflect on the things you are grateful for can help you shift your focus away from what's going wrong in your life, and toward the positive things that bring you joy and peace.

Remember, finding inner peace is a journey and what works for one person may not work for another. It's important to try out different techniques and find what works best for you. With regular practice and a commitment to self-care, you can develop a sense of inner peace and contentment that lasts a lifetime

<u>Building a daily mindfulness practic. Encouragement for continued growth and self-discovery.</u>

<u>e</u>

Building a daily mindfulness practice can be a powerful tool for unlocking your inner potential and finding greater peace and happiness. Here are some steps to help you get started:

Set aside a specific time each day for your mindfulness practice: Choose a time of day when you are most alert and have the least amount of distractions, such as first thing in the morning or last thing at night. Make this time a priority and stick to it as consistently as possible.

Start with just a few minutes: Mindfulness can be intimidating at first, but it's important to start with just a few minutes each day and gradually increase the amount of time you spend in mindfulness as you become more comfortable with the practice.

Choose a focus: Whether it's your breath, a mantra, or a body scan, choose a focus for your mindfulness practice and return to it whenever your mind begins to wander. This can help you stay present and grounded in the moment.

Practice non-judgment: One of the key elements of mindfulness is to observe your thoughts and feelings without judgment. This can be challenging, but it's important to cultivate a sense of curiosity and openness to your experience, rather than getting caught up in negativity or criticism.

Make it a habit: The more you practice mindfulness, the more natural and effortless it will become. Make it a habit by incorporating it into your daily routine, such as before or after a meal, or after a specific activity.

Be patient: Building a daily mindfulness practice takes time and effort, but the benefits are well worth it. Be patient with yourself and don't get discouraged if it feels challenging at first. With consistent practice, you'll find that mindfulness becomes easier and more natural over time.

Incorporating mindfulness into your daily routine can have a profound impact on your life. It can help you cultivate greater self-awareness, reduce stress and anxiety, and improve your overall well-being. So, start small and make mindfulness a daily habit, and you'll soon experience the ultimate benefits of unlocking your true self.

<u>Understanding the power of gratitude</u>

Gratitude is a powerful tool for unlocking the full potential of the human experience. By focusing on the things we are thankful for, we can shift our perspective and gain a deeper appreciation for life's blessings. Here are some ways to understand the power of gratitude:

<u>Promotes Positive Thinking</u>: Gratitude helps us focus on the positive aspects of our lives, which can help us develop a more optimistic outlook. By recognizing the good things in our lives, we can counteract negative thoughts and feelings, and cultivate a greater sense of happiness and well-being.

<u>Increases Resilience</u>: When we practice gratitude, we are less likely to become overwhelmed by the challenges and

difficulties we face. Instead, we are more likely to approach adversity with a positive attitude, which can help us overcome obstacles more easily and bounce back from setbacks.

Improves Relationships: Gratitude can help improve relationships by promoting positive feelings and reducing negativity. When we focus on what we appreciate about others, we are more likely to foster healthy, supportive relationships, and to feel more connected to those around us.

Enhances Physical Health: Research has shown that gratitude can have a positive impact on physical health, including lower levels of stress, improved sleep, and a stronger immune system. By focusing on what we are grateful for, we can boost our physical and emotional well-being.

Deepens Spiritual Connection: Gratitude can deepen our spiritual connection by helping us see the interconnectedness of all things and the blessings in our lives. By recognizing the gifts and blessings in our lives, we can develop a deeper sense of purpose and a stronger connection to something greater than ourselves.

Incorporating gratitude into your daily life can be as simple as taking a few moments each day to reflect on what you are thankful for. Whether it's through journaling, speaking with loved ones, or simply taking a moment to reflect, gratitude has the power to unlock your full potential and bring greater meaning and happiness to your life.

ChapterIX

. Conclusion

In summary, "Unlocking Your Ultimate Self" offers valuable perspectives and direction for individuals seeking to explore themselves and develop personally. By highlighting the key principles of self-awareness, personal growth, positive mindset, healthy habits, mindfulness, emotional intelligence, and purpose, the book offers a roadmap for unlocking your full potential and living a fulfilling life.

As you continue on your journey, it's important to remember that self-discovery is an ongoing process that requires dedication, effort, and a willingness to grow and learn. Whether you are just starting out or are well on your way, this book provides a useful and inspiring resource for anyone seeking to unlock their ultimate self. So, take heart, stay committed to your journey, and never stop striving towards becoming the best version of your self.

www.ingramcontent.com/pod-product-compliance
Lightning Source LLC
Chambersburg PA
CBHW081830250726
48653CB00017B/3875